Kristen Stewart
Twilight Star

Maggie Murphy

PowerKiDS press.

New York

Published in 2011 by The Rosen Publishing Group, Inc.
29 East 21st Street, New York, NY 10010

First Edition

Book Design: Greg Tucker
Photo Researcher: Jessica Gerweck

Photo Credits: Cover John Shearer/WireImage/Getty Images; p. 5 Jeffrey
Mayer/WireImage/Getty Images; pp. 7, 15 Kevin Mazur/WireImage/
Getty Images; p. 8–9 Lester Cohen/WireImage/Getty Images; p. 11 ©
Twilight Productions; p. 13 Todd Williamson/WireImage/Getty Images;
p. 17 George Pimentel/WireImage/Getty Images; p. 19 Carlos Alvarez/
Getty Images; pp. 20–21 Kevin Winter/Getty Images; p. 22 Gustavo
Caballero/Getty Images.

Library of Congress Cataloging-in-Publication Data

Murphy, Maggie.
  Kristen Stewart : twilight star / Maggie Murphy. — 1st ed.
    p. cm. — (Young and famous)
  Includes index.
  ISBN 978-1-4488-0641-6 (library binding) —
ISBN 978-1-4488-1795-5 (pbk.) — ISBN 978-1-4488-1796-2 (6-pack)
  1. Stewart, Kristen, 1990—Juvenile literature. 2. Actors—United
States—Biography—Juvenile literature. I. Title.
  PN2287.S685M87 2011
  791.4302'8092—dc22
  [B]
                              2009050870

Manufactured in the United States of America

CPSIA Compliance Information: Batch #WS10PK: For Further Information contact Rosen Publishing, New York, New York at
1-800-237-9932

Contents

Kristen Stewart is a movie star. She was born on April 9, 1990.

Kristen lives in Los Angeles, California. Many movie stars live there.

Kristen stars in the *Twilight* movies. These movies made her **famous**.

She plays the **role** of Bella Swan. Bella falls in love with a **vampire**.

Kristen also starred in *Adventureland*.

13

She has won **awards** for her acting. She won a 2009 MTV Movie Award.

15

Kristen likes to sing
and play the guitar.

Kristen is friends with Taylor Lautner. Many of her other friends are actors, too.

19

Kristen has
many fans.

Kristen loves to act.
She will be a star for
a long time!

Books

Here are more books to read about Kristen Stewart:

Hurley, Jo. *Kristen Stewart: Bella of the Ball.* New York: Scholastic, Inc., 2009.

Orr, Tamra. *Kristen Stewart.* Blue Banner Biographies. Hockessin, DE: Mitchell Lane Publishers, 2009.

Web Sites

Due to the changing nature of Internet links, PowerKids Press has developed an online list of Web sites related to the subject of this book. This site is updated regularly. Please use this link to access the list:
www.powerkidslinks.com/young/ks/

Glossary

awards (uh-WORDZ) Honors given to people.

famous (FAY-mus) Very well known.

role (ROHL) A part played by a person in a movie, TV show, or play.

vampire (VAM-py-er) A dead person in stories and folktales who drinks blood.

Index